Alan grew up in the suburbs of Pittsburgh, PA, where he was introduced to the arts by his mother. He attended West Virginia University, where he graduated with a degree in political science. He's called Lancaster, PA, his home for the past 25 years. When not working at the lock shop, he spends his time writing with his granddaughter, and his best friend, Patch, his dog.

I dedicate this book to my mother and father, June and Larry Silverman, and my sisters, Susan Marrone and Amy Sukay. Growing up in this family was the greatest gift.

Alan P. Silverman

THOUGHTS UNLOCKED

Poetry from a Locksmith

AUSTIN MACAULEY PUBLISHERS™

LONDON · CAMBRIDGE · NEW YORK · SHARJAH

Ordering Information
Quantity sales: Special discounts are available on quantity purchases by corporations, associations, and others. For details, contact the publisher at the address below.

Publisher's Cataloging-in-Publication data
Silverman, Alan P.
Thoughts Unlocked

ISBN 9781647503260 (Paperback)
ISBN 9781647503277 (Hardback)
ISBN 9781647503284 (ePub e-book)

Library of Congress Control Number: 2022911533

www.austinmacauley.com/us

First Published 2022
Austin Macauley Publishers LLC
40 Wall Street, 33rd Floor, Suite 3302
New York, NY 10005
USA

mail-usa@austinmacauley.com
+1 (646) 5125767

I'd like to thank Austin Macauley Publishers for publishing this book of poetry. In addition, I thank the butterfly. From caterpillar to free winged spirit its metamorphosis taught me that change is beautiful. That's why I write.

Table of Contents

Foreword

Sunday,
it's hours move too fast.
A garden harvested before the heat.
Coffee, black.

The day's news tiresome.
Some music and reading.
The laborious week ahead in view
 time moving forward.
Napping, unrealistic... it steals from the day.

I've taken to writing, where the minutes last longer. A
timeless world.
Every stroke of the pen a painters canvass, every word
toiled over to complete the picture.
At final punctuation, a smile on my face. Time briefly
forgotten.

Morning's harvest is prepared for dinner.
My companion by my side, his eye's focused, tail wagging
in anticipation.
We share a meal.
How fortunate for him to not be chained to time.

Of Life

Figment

Presume me alive if my thoughts linger aimlessly between reality and imagination. It is the dead that think in black and white. Artless, will be the death of us all. Figment with no boundary, full of color, distorted illusions and unattainable glory feeds the desires of life. It is this, not the drums of war, not the quest for possession, and not the quest of power that drives existence.

Traveled

I have traveled less but have breathed the air and soil of foreign lands, conquered the highest peaks, battled rugged terrain, gazed at breathtaking architecture, breathed the bouquet of indigenous flowers, sung the songs of locals, tasted the fruit and bread, held the hands of lost souls and lonely children, visited the newborn, paid final respects, seen the effects of war... just as real as you, through well-written chapters.

Sing

Sing to the wind and rain and in return your song will be carried through orchard, through mountain and uncharted waters. Its lyrics spread among the hillside's flowers; it is melody to the yearning ears of Earth. Carried to the heavens, it comforts those gone with captive tempo. Hovering above clouds, waiting to share with the future. Shout your song, the rain will end soon.

Spoil

So often in the valley where my thoughts rest, a vision of a coarse and rambling sea appears in fashion with forlorn memory of a distant fading call to chivalry.

It is there that I can conquer any setback. Closed eyes, clenched fists, can fight through raging pain. The sunset often comes before the day's dawn, where the spirit stays dry from laughing rain.

My venture once assembled takes me outward to the final ledge that sits beyond the pale of nature's quest to find the answer's glory, to the questions we've spilled blood known all too well.

A setback looms before my final hour, to the east I look for unknown facts that spoil truth. Awoken from a river's bed of darkness, shaking from the mind that's turned me loose.

Puppet

Tired, not form the tasks or the day said the puppet, but from always being told what to do. Tonight, I sever the controlling hand, standing on my own, free from bent knuckles. The words I speak will come from my own tongue, not of villainous voice. I will speak of truth. If I fail, I would rather lie in shackled chest collecting dust than to cover a well-bruised hand once again.

Poetry

Captured shakes in tired hands too painful to slow down.
Fueled by innocence of thought buried in the ground.
Question asked at midnight's moon, reflective not on script.
Things I once held tight to breast have fallen loose from grip.

Philosophers in carnival steady to explain.
Meaning of complex life across the fruited plain.
Was he who twisted words of thought to penetrate the weak?
Fallen from the forward mind, I've nothing left to seek.

Corners torn on picture aged faded from the years.
Fortress faint from eroding strength and flowing heartfelt tears.
The sun confused by daily toll has settled in the east.
Decision born from timely prayer and the murder of the beast.

Self-taught smile from poetry emancipates the mind.
From words of thorny walk through green and trees of every kind.

Escaping from a blemished start that lies beyond the star.
Writing down in syllables, the dream is not that far.

Perception

We each walk in our own world, perceiving the trees differently. To you shade, to me, it blocks the sun. Your God heals, while mine sits by and watches misery and death. Your rain floods and ruins, mine gives life to flowers. Your sky heaven, mine endless space of opportunity. Your money to buy gems, mine to feed the poor.

Nomad

Observant to nothing, the nomad lived a harmonious life. No land to die for, guilt from refusing to bow. Her Sunday full of fruits and wine. Returning the borrowed air to feed her lungs, her only contract with nature. Beautiful visions and sounds she witnessed, her stage. With no language, never a painful word spoken to another. But love she could express through shimmering eyes and smile, which she spread infinitely. Sheltered by internal rainbow, she lived a life of peace.

Cinnamon

Broken sky, fallen river, fog has settled thick.

Charmed cadence, skips in time, patterned, homeward bound.

Winds accelerate, gray abound, trouble in the wilderness.

Hat blown away, ribbon of red soars in distant view. Tears dry before touched by cheek.

Door open, corralled by open arms of mother, cinnamon in the air.

Morning sun, dried earth, daisy reaches out to say hello.

Far away, little girl with smile puts on her newly found hat of red ribbon.

Crash

Certain colors only seen with eyes closed, not fitting in the normal palette, paint the walls of wonders, hope and escape. Their definition sharp, depth endless. Overwhelming with appeal, they crash through borders unselfishly, sharing radiant pouring not from words... from mind's eye. Free from the painter's hand, free from restrictive brush.

Culture

A world without culture, boundaries and pedestals is a world of peace.

Crooked Time

Beyond the steps of ego's mind, the gatekeeper loses pace.
Out into forbidden land, a path that leaves no trace.
Its forest full of dangers smile, response not found, farewell.
The streets are paved with tortured land, neglect, no one can tell.

Shadows form on hill of dirt, they can't be seen, no sun.
Death of life begins to live; saints begin to run.
Water flows in crooked time, no splash to indicate,
The drowning of the self-made man to which he's lost his fate.

The wind, it blows with hardened breath, it penetrates the sphere,
Of lover's hurt too many times, succumb to lonely fear.
The trees they grow with branchless limbs, trunks too weak to hold,
Stories of endangered young, and the thinning of the old.

Ark

There's no room left, your future is dark,
The flood has started, no room on the ark.
Gather your soldiers, with guns in hands,
We'll take from another and invade their land.

We'll kill them slowly without hesitation,
Incarcerate them on their own reservation.
We'll get some slaves to plow the fields,
Keep them in line, the mighty whip wields.

Craft paper of rights and laws a must.
No matter how wrong, in God we trust.
The sins of a nation since its time of birth,
Normalized each Sunday in the pews of a church.

Lucy

Lucy dances to the sound of the wind, her movement slow and pristine,
Buttoned collar, flared jeans, a smile you've never seen. The music she hears is not of this world, it's melody from endless sky.
Through notes unheard from distant realm, she sways in perfect time.

Storyteller pen in hand sits on bank of creek.
A dancer to tell story of is what she'll try to seek.
Wind picks up as night moves in no words as she forgets.
Lucy does pirouette with no one watching yet.

Distant ship on voyage rough to edge of mind's escape.
Current strong, rain pours down, as it navigates.
While Lucy shines unto herself a flawless diamond bright.
Another story never told, as ship sails through the night.

Meadow

At night I sit in the lonely corner of this old musty house. The only sound is the harmony created by the rocking chair and the involuntary movement of my feet to keep them warm. A symphony would be nice; I will have to settle for this simple arrangement though. The soft light of a candle allows me to see the picture of a meadow in the opposing corner only, nothing else. Although void of color, that meadow is all I can see. It is my companion until dawn when the sun fills my room. Until then, I am void of any joyful thoughts. My mind is cluttered with past deaths, past relationships, missed opportunities and downtrodden occasions. As these thoughts swell, I try to think positive, but like an insect on its back trying to turn over, I am unsuccessful. The candle is slowly burning down and as it gasps for its last breath, I stare at the meadow one last time as its presence vanishes into the night with the soft burning smell of the candle's death. To gain composure, I change my rocking pattern and the timing of my pitter patter. It keeps me occupied for a few minutes, but eventually, the negative thoughts overwhelm me once again. Without the meadow to see and my rhythmic patterns exhausted, I sit with eyes wide open, shivering with undesirable thoughts.

The next three hours, excruciating. I sit with my hands hanging to my side, cold and unhappy with a single tear rolling down my cheek. With no strength to wipe it from my face, it evaporates into the air. With my head hanging low, I notice a ray. I can see particles of dust in that ray. Soon enough, my meadow will be back. And as I see it, the rest of the musty room awakens. I get up from my chair, put on my coat and walk to work. As I pass others on the street, we pleasantly exchange "good mornings", and move on. I pause for a second and wonder if they are fortunate enough as I to have a meadow to look at every night.

Storied Life

The clock is ticking, up on the painted wall.
Its hands are meek and it's ready to take a fall.
It's kept good, metered time, all though the waning years.
Its seconds running out of space, it has too much to bear.

Down the musty hall sits the faded rocking chair.
With its broken back, it sits in ill-repair.
Its legs are weakened by the comfort that it gave.
And the creaks have loudly sounded, from the cradle to the grave.

Inside the mildewed washroom, the sink has washed away tears,
From the faces of the children, as it calmed their many fears.
And the mirror poised above it has captured many eyes.
The reflection that harbors is filled with patron's cries.

So proudly to protect, as the hinges hold the front door.
While the splinters from its years of use, lie softly on the floor.

It's protected from the world outside, from people and the cold.
And the house has lived its own storied life, a story seldom told.

God Is in the Bleachers

Well God is in the bleachers, with his popcorn in his hand,
Thinking 'bout the rage he had, and the time he flooded land.
A lesson he didn't teach too well, in fact his judgment poor,
He should of spoke in peaceful terms, not of death and war.

A little girl beside herself, she's got no one to blame.
She's been searching for the land of Oz and figuring out the game.
But with no one to talk to, her parents not around,
So she just sits patiently, with the scarecrow on the ground.

Here come the nonprofit charities, with their buckets and their tears.
Trying to patch lives together, that have been destroyed for years.
And then they send the precious money, to those immersed in need,
But don't forget to take their cut, with pockets full of greed.

And then the politicians, with their smiles so bright and white.
You should see the liar's face, it's not so bright at night.
As they're mixing up their poison, to infect your mind,
You sleep so comfortably, as they undo mankind.

Then the crazy aliens, from a far and distant place,
Rejoice, laugh, dance and sing, with joy upon their face.
And as they stare down at us, with anger, toil and boiling blood.
They wish that God had got it right, and never caused a flood.

And then the lonely poet, sits with paper and his pen,
Stares at neatly placed words, and says he'll never write again.

But then loneliness blankets him, he has so much to say.
And then the words paint pictures of life, as they're pouring off the page.

Faucet

The faucet fights to pour out water as we tighten it to close.
Its final drips are tears, saddened as it no longer flows.
Strangulated by our hands, its river ceases to pour.
The pain it holds in captivity lies lifeless beneath the floor.

Somewhere in a far-off place, a child is told to hush,
For no uncertain reason, maybe mother is in a rush.
All the little one wants to do, is express their essential view.
So extremely important to them, but not to me and you.

The child goes off in the corner, shut from the world again.
Children should be seen not heard, to speak out of turn is a
sin.
A most ridiculous cliché that has endured the test of time,
I'll never understand its worth, to constrict a young one's
mind.

The child upon its step stool washing up at night,
Tears rolling down their cheek as they turn the faucet tight.

Storyteller

With your gravel voice, you tell your tale, of mystery, deception and fate.
Your audience on every word, with yearning anticipate.
Your story shifts from romantic verses to a baby's lullaby.
A turn you make to pull on heartstrings, including those to cry.

A whirlwind masquerade takes places, as you describe it with your voice.
Pageantry and colors galore describe it best by choice.
Squalls of rain, pouring down at sea from heavens up above.
The catalyst for a drowning soul, the one the captain loved.

Shifting to an island, with beach and drink and sun.
The audience with smiles on face, embracing in the fun.
Next, the frightful passage, the one that makes you shiver.
As the sight monsters eating brains, will surely make you quiver.

A tale of war is shared with all, a painful, courageous fight.
Tears on cheeks around the room, like it happens every night.
The audience, with puzzled look, the storyteller talks no more.
His breathing strained and shallow, as he lies upon the floor.
No tale of love, or mystery, no tale of a treasure chest.
His final story ended, doing what he loved to do best.

Deliver

What a cowardly sentiment to perpetuate, seeing loved ones after death, only to lie in eternal darkness. Gather your flowers and deliver now, they cannot be seen nor does their fragrance penetrate the perished. Procrastinate not, the risk is too great.

Watchman

Endless sounds of half scoffed tongues too dangerous to hear.
Shrouded by a whispered cry, conclusions softly stare.
Through flaming rails of eternity, I travel with soul on loan.
The quiet beat rings loud in brain when standing all alone.

The horseman sit side saddled, with fraught and anchored fears.
Wise men fail to pass the test, but blanket world with fear.
Trumpet plays the minor keys, as the book reveals it plot.
Tempered fight cascading slow, the watchman loses thought.

Vase

The broken vase no longer holds water, its cracks too much to bear.

Its shattered heart holds on by thread, its friend, a lonely tear.

The glass that once was strong and thick has weakened from within. A tiny pebble with piercing words had broken through its skin.

No sutures of repair can help, it is lonely by itself.

It clings to life painfully as it teeters on the shelf.

Tombstone

Persuasive yawns of tired thought,
Plead selfish sleep while graveyards rot.
Their carved-out names will disappear,
Depth of letters are just a mere.
Reflection of days gone by,
Those who visit no longer cry.

Pendulum

Your mind's pendulum continues to sway to the weep of the dying willow branch. Reminiscing in yesterday's failures and expectations. It draws its pattern over and over in your mind's sand, waiting for a gentle shake to change its course.

Oasis

Walking along the ledge with dangling outer foot, inside clenched to ground. A stroll with no coherent physical destination, only a mental one to free the mind. Danger present but needed, keeping coordination in balance while the mind wonders. Carved in stone to my right, I pass a pledge of love where lovers once walked, date unknown. Are they dead, happy, apart? At least for that moment, the world was good to them. A soaring hawk to my left carrying a lifeless squirrel, on way to perch to feast. His belly full now, the squirrel no longer exists, nature can be harsh. A bead of sweat falls from brow. I stumble, losing battle with cliff, falling, fate doomed, only to land upon oasis of books. Forgotten ones, purged by man. I remained there the rest of my days, intrigued, reading my way down to the last one. With shaky hand, I turned to the last page of the final book. Its only sentence read, "Even a carving in stone doesn't last forever." As I took my last breath, I mourned the squirrel's death.

Negativity

Tirades of capture escape through a whim,
Legs struggle to posture, future looks dim.
Your street has been conquered with a furious gait.
Penetrated by destiny, it is never too late.

The white dove lands on the seal of window,
It replaces the sadness of the withering crow.

Once shut eyes from a torrent event,
Have softly opened, from a message sent.
The dove delivers the needed embrace,
To your heart it delivers sanctuary and grace.

Legs are poised to deliver your thoughts,
While the crow has died, negativity rots.

Negative

Raging trails in paths unknown lie dormant in heaven's atmosphere.
Tried by explorers from antiquity with limited *navigation* and fear.
Pressured by insanity that breeds within their thought.
Gallantly fall upon their sword, salvation cannot be bought.

Tethered minds to vacant half climbed hills look backwards to the ground.
Searching for original sin, only never to be found.
Historical trains scream loud and clear from strong and sturdy rail.
To the West they hear but ignore in vain, conscience has lost appeal.

In the mirrored house with doors closed shut a reflection of eternity.
The image stands in combative stance, a fight between he and me.
My shield fallen flat; I swing my arms to protect myself from me.
To no avail, I lose again, my reflection running free.

The acrobat twists and turns, has struggled with an ailing stance.

Her foot has weakened and left her crying, a struggling circumstance.

With power inside she fights through pain, with laughter she executes flip.

Fortitude weighs heavily, as she *navigates* her ship.

Library

Summer night, the depths of August, I build a wall around my mind's castle. Sweat pouring from skin, wiping my brow, the final brick placed in. It holds safe, I am protected from the world, lounging in my universe. One hand relaxed and weak in stature, the other clenched and poised to fracture. No partitions to skew privacy, nothing to hide but emotions. The grass grows but not green. Void of sun, brown is all that is seen. The lack of color does not disappoint, a reminder that not everything flourishes. It grants perspective and unobstructed views. No rainbow to whitewash, no philosophy to choose. The sundries minimal. Its picture frames empty, its clock with no hands. There is nothing to distract my mind. The outside world violent and rude, where inside the world is kind. Books aplenty fill its library. Volumes from antiquity until now. The poetic verses of yesterday's thought bring me clarity for things that I have sought. The castle temporary but worth the labor. Its environment friendly. Its umbrella shields from pain and trick. My muscles ache, mind feels heavy, I reach for another brick.

Lessons

Countless gains on fields of life, turned back from day's routine.
Obstacles of well-thought plans, lie dormant in a changing scene.
Surrounded by sage's words, meaning often misconstrued.
Perception runs through muddy lake, allegory poorly used.

Time halts within lover's choice, they choose to slow it down.
While time speeds through the lonely branch, its roots cannot be found.
Flowers penetrate the song; its melody sets sail to stern.
Rainbows wash away the rain, lessons never learned.

Good Friend

Out of the sea the poem surfaces, its words brought up from
below.
It speaks of lives submerged forever, where no man dares to
go.
Where creatures care to tell the truth, of love and war they
write.
Void of pen and paper, as well as any light.

They write in ways not understood by man's inferior brain.
Poems of magnificent places, some poems filled with pain.
The water keeps these words submerged, no one gets to see.
My mermaid friend had lost her life, for sharing them with
me.

Firefly

Turn back the time to yesterday,
Where the sun shined more, where we played all day.
When the swing at the park got us high,
And the carousel dizzy, that we used to ride.

The sky told us time from the angle of the sun,
It's time for dinner, I better run.
I could smell the cooking up and down the street,
Washed my hands and took my seat.

"I washed the dishes; I finished my chore."
"OK," Mom said, I was out the door.
One last time to the field I went,
With friends from the neighborhood, time well spent.

The sun would fall, as we said goodbye,
Then we would catch our last firefly.
I would make my way, back to home,
By myself but never alone.

Fangs

Pictures frames with nothing to hold, their corners too obtuse,
Canvass filled with colored life; their frays have become loose.
Countless words put down by pen, meaning lost today,
Windowsill dust still there, the rag was thrown away.

Walls of plaster chipped away, cracks like rivers grow.
Mirror holds reflections of pain from long ago.
Weathered facts that once were true melt from biased heat.
Precious fangs from carnivores still tearing at the meat.

Musty smells of attic old, penetrate the blind.
Closet doors nailed tightly shut, asphyxiate the mind.
Timber thrown on fireplace with memories of old.
Standing in this homeless house with nothing left to hold.

Of Nature

Fragile

I climbed the tree only to find the view was no better. The path was easier to navigate but the challenge was negated, leaving me disappointed. No flowers to smell. No rocks to climb. No stream to wade. No shade to protect. No ground to rest. The limbs atop the tree were fragile, offering no hope of security. I will remain grounded and only see what is meant for me to see.

Stream

The stream's determination mightier than the ocean. Its boundaries well-defined between the jagged rocks. Survival dependent on constant flow, a tired soul she is. Her trickle musical, feel crisp, taste pure. With drought comes death, her will hovering above waiting for sky to feed. In time, she will reincarnate, fresh lavender by her side, tall grass to protect.

Fawn, Sparrow, Fish

Breathe in the future air and step upon the blades of grass that hold no dew. Let the others cry their tears of nature, a renewal much needed. Let the rose remain steadfast to the thorny bush. Their contradiction more beautiful than dead petals in palms. Let the hills keep their trails and peaks. The hearts they fill outweigh the need of market. Let the brooks run their course along the mountainside. They feed the fawn, the sparrow and breathe life into fish. Let the poet dream and the philosopher think, let the antagonists say farewell.

Airborne

Sitting at the breakfast table, warm rays of sun light up the room, the smell of morning all around, I finish my juice with no plan for the day.

The flowers outside my door have a slight bend, especially the red ones, "Is the breeze too strong, or are they just being lazy? Why the red and not the yellow, the yellow looking healthy?"

Birds swim flawlessly, sky their ocean, ground their table. The worm enjoying the mud until its final destiny. Finally, airborne in belly of bird, cost is death.

A great storm ensues, I watch from the window. Limbs torn from crying tree. Foundation uprooted, falling on flowers. Red ones escape, the bend, their shield, yellow ones crushed, morning is over.

Lonely Jupiter

Moonlight has risen, it is the end of the day.
My mind lives in vacuum, with nothing to say.
Bones are on empty, there is a calm in the air.
World is on fire, why should I care?

Nottingham Forest still holds the purse.
Robin Hood's fortune was never dispersed.
People live vaguely, they are on bended knees.
The forest has nothing, but old rotted trees.

Jupiter's lonely, but rules endless sky.
Earth's deeds are captured, with its vast orange eye.
Saturn its partner, plays piano and sings.
While Jupiter hovers and stares at her rings.

Book lost its cover; words still ring true.
Meaning of life has been misconstrued.
Shadows have covered a once open place.
Nothing makes sense, but the lines on my face.

The Poet Rose

The lines are drawn to a new portrait with pastels undiscovered, bright. Do not write of love, its mundane verse regurgitated endlessly. Write of color, spirit, wind and adventure. Share those elements with the world, like the rose does. Its deep red, willingness to withstand storm, carried fragrance. It is truly a spectacular poet, all to learn from.

Won't Kill

Not for any reason other than I like stars, I keep my head tilted upward at night. The wings of evening's creatures lights atop a city building, the clock-tower in the square, the moon above, the taillights of steel birds all pale to the old but never tiring drama above as Orion goes on his daily hunt. With his spirit balanced, patience in stature, sword poised above, he has yet to kill, but always ready. Where does he find his strength to continue? I will look up again tonight, maybe this is the night his sword turns red.

The Gardener

In the distant horizon of the mind, deep in its hidden abyss where things just tend to lay dormant, never acted upon but always have a strong presence, lives the seed never watered. And so, the gardener tries her best, but a great drought endures for years leaving a barren environment in which nothing can be nurtured. The land turned and cultivated year after year with no results. With shivers and unpleasantness, the gardener, her eyes closed floats away on her own stream of tears. Her eyes full and nowhere for the tears to fall, a single tear takes a different path, finding its way deep inside her mind. At last, a tiny green stem appears.

Clinging

Sitting in the old bay window, watching the icicle falling ill,
Clinging on as best as it can, the sun imposes its will.
Never giving up too much, its lifeline one drop at a time.
It fights the penetrating rays, its courage greater than yours
and mine.

With gutters happy as they have less stress, the icicle
tightens down its grip.
The sun's rays softening close to dusk, it cannot afford one
more drip.
The horizon has swallowed the evil sun, and temperatures
have chilled the air,
The mighty icicle survived the day, it can sleep with no
threat or fear.

Spectacular Bird

Whisk me away upon your wings, spectacular bird, so I may leave the shackles of the ground and feel freedom. Take me through the clouds, upward, to the perfect shade of blue, high above where serenity exists. Let me pause for a moment or two so I may clear my thoughts and void any pain. Take me to the highest mountain top where I can taste pure water from an endless stream and cleanse my soul. Let me sleep under the stars and dream of lavender and breezes. When I awake, hoist me in your wings and take me back to my crowded, polluted and noisy place. There is still work to be done.

Antique Compass

No antique compass to point my way back.
An unwanted memory has thrown me off track.

The town has emptied with friends dispersed wide,
While the buzzards are circling above in the sky.

The water lies stagnant in a pond of remorse.
The stars misaligned have thrown me off course.

The bridge to the outskirts no longer exists.
My mind says move forward, but my heart persists.

I dig through the shattered rubble of time.
My muscles failing, I am out of my prime.

The shovel itself bears too much weight.
The moon fills the sky, I have started too late.

Poised on my feet, I search for trees.
I knelt in great pain from my two labored knees.

The sun rose slowly, in pain as it climbed.
It too gets weary with no reason or rhyme.

But it fights through its hurt every day to provide,
The light that is needed for us to survive.

Back on my feet, my gait off, unstable.
I pick up the shovel as good as I'm able.
Through the rubble I plow for things from the past.
With the strength from the sun, I just hope that it lasts.

Tangerine

"Tangerine is my favorite color," she said,
"A shade less than orange, and not bold like red.
It reminds me of a soft shimmering light,
It too brings comfort that is not too bright.
It is a delicate fruit, handled hard will bruise,
Its flavor delicious, it is the fruit that I choose.
Unlike its nemesis, the peach with its fuzz,
It tastes so much better, trust me it does.
Although I am tempted by the apple of green,
Its taste somewhat sour, its worms obscene.
The sweet taste of banana brings mass appeal,
But its cover brings danger, do not slip on its peel.
And the grapes too have taste that we all want and need,
Be careful my friend, do not choke on the seed.
The mango a favorite of many well-fit,
It too presents danger, don't swallow the pit.
Many to choose from, from red, blue and green,
She will stick with her favorite, the great tangerine."

Impatient

Be it the green in morning,
Be it the orange at nightfall,
The bark remains calm,
Not uttering a word,
But learning each day quietly,
Strengthening itself below the soil,
Slowly stretching towards sky,
Will one day touch the stars,
While its impatient leaves
Are carried away by the wind.

Gift

Shake a fist at the iron wind, and fight 'till breath is dim.
The battle cry is at your door, exhaust everything within.
Do not speak of love at this time of need, let it drown in
river deep.
If true love you have inside, gather and put to sleep.

The world awaits your gift of art, poetry, paint and song.
Cast your gift into the wind, dream subdued too long.
When fight is over, wounds have healed, validation you
craved is earned.
Search riverbed for once held love and hope it will return.

Gate

Rusty gate dressed in ivy, its outward creak a path to beyond. Violet field seduces, cleansed thoughts await the weary. Water's trickle warms the bones through endless miracle of endless splash. Carried by breeze, the primrose announces its presence, not shy to invade. Creatures dance sporadically, offending not their neighbor, keeping to their possession of nature. Inward creak of gate, enchanted world gone for day. Current path barren until diversion taken again. Looking back at swaying tree.

Garden of Weeds

The most abrasive hurtful words are the ones put to paper, never spoken. They lie in your mind's coffin, sealed indefinitely. Begged to the heard, haunting for your future, protecting your past, inevitably causing discomfort. Journeyed to tongue's tip, always ending there, solemn return to gut. They live through solitude, dream and fantasy with no risk. Not ready for tainted world. Their syllables perfect, phrasing brilliant... their stage's curtain drawn, theater empty, tucked away in garden of weeds internal.

Destination

If sky is cluttered by clouds of persuasion, leaving moon, sun and stars vulnerable as a compass, I will choose the wind, fallen leaves and trickling water as my guides. The wind to carry my imagination, the crackle of the leaves to assure solid ground, sound of stream to keep my spirit close to unwavering fish, the ultimate survivor. The green of the countryside will fill my wonder, its blossom my senses, its bend flowing to final destination.

Bird

What a sad affair to be a bird. Most jealous of its flight, not realizing the horrible view of war, death and toil it sees in its vast scenery. Its dream, to be flightless, immune like others by restrictive landscape.

Stench

Green field in memory from a distant mind's dream.
Unheard responses from questions between,
Flowing ripples from the lake of concern.
Timely answers patiently learned.

Back towards vengeance, escaped from it all.
Rehearse the excuse, predictable fall.
Unfriendly chatter, behind hills of despair.
Pretentious filter, there is a stench in the air.

Time predicts heaven, loners unite.
Unwanted feelings, through pain and fright.
Forward steps taken, slowly through storm.
Masses are hurting, above, vultures swarm.

Neglected Fortress

Wind, rain and letters stolen from wretched hearts tumble towards neglected fortress that once protected. As the rain softens the corridor, the wind divides and conquers making way for past letters to form those refused lessons. Unconquered fears remain inescapable.

Soar

Flourish through the night my wind, take your captive dance,
Swirl above the lavender, the smell of sweet romance.
Turnabout in gala style, pageantry for midnight air,
Carry with you breath of life, to those in great despair.
Circle about the heavens north, leave a tear for me,
Soar through storm to mountain top, above the calming sea.
Lie still at ocean's beach, pause at lonely shore,
Grasp the spirit from sunrise gold, deliver to my door.

Strong Gust

Pleased by the calming words she spoke, the keeper of the wind rested for a while. No bent branches, no ripples in lake, no traveling smell of comfort. For that day, this strength was not needed, his lungs on holiday of wishes, to forever hear her voice… She missed the breeze that carried her ambitions and spoke in tongue of conscience. The keeper disappointed, blew strong gust. Ambitious she now was but carried away by strong current.

Weeds

With back bent, the tall weeds fight against the storm. They struggle to survive. Victorious, they sway softly, antagonizing the neighboring flowers uprooted and colorless. A solitary weed breathes life into one. Soon a garden of vibrancy flourishes. The weeds left hoping for storm.

Etiquette

Fiery red shards from inner voice, too hurtful to take heed.
Endless pranks on jagged edge, stable land that I need.
It was you that said I need not try, for glory or for fame.
My ears were shut from infected words, I suppose it is all
the same.

Circle runs inside the square of eternal wants and needs.
Punished by the guillotine of romantic wants and deeds.
The breath of vulture breathes its scorn on fields of carcass
hell.
While rainbow fades dramatically, the drought has dried the
well.

Sunshine glows on plowed fields' skin, burning deep in soil.
River carries lovers' pain along with all its toil.
Shepherd's skill has lost its source, his mind has gone
astray.
The sheep have broken etiquette, they have all gone off to
play.

Fragrant fields of well-grown flowers, fill lungs with poetry.

Mind has traveled to mountaintop and through the raging sea.

The scent has stained my inner thought, all throughout the year.

Sound returned to daily life; pain is gone from ear.

For Jayliana

Sleep

Let them sleep.
Through war.
Through sickness.
Through hunger.
Through pain.
Let them dream fields of violets,
warm breezes, carousels and flowers of candy.
"Cling to the blanket with your small hands, it will comfort
you. Wake when ready to make your dreams come true."
For now, let them sleep.

Granddaughter

In the middle of a step,
a fraction before my right foot dusted the grass,
it came to me.

Small hand reaching out,
finding mine easily,
eternal smiles.

Feeling enlightened,
euphoria penetrating memory,
encased in peace.

Mutual step taken,
grass felt between toes,
granddaughter's love.

Your Land of Flavor

Raspberry speckles in pools filled with cream,
Clouds made of rainbows that cover your dream.
Streets that are lined with lollipop lights.
They taste sweet and yummy and light up the nights.

A lake full of chocolate, both milk and dark,
And trees so tasty, you can eat their bark.
An ocean of flavor of cherry and peach,
With watermelon flowers that grow on the beach.

Where grass is green with apple taste.
Everything's beautiful with nothing to waste.
Your land of flavor with ice cream pies,
Is waiting for you when you close your eyes.

Utter

They were not words thrown into the wind.
They were carefully chosen, every syllable.
Some natural and some difficult to speak.
They were words of solace,
Meant to dwell on,
Meant to rely upon,
And meant to guide.
From a skinned knee,
To when you utter similar words,
In the future.

Sunday

I have a little one, she brings me lots of fun, she stands in her beautiful dress.
It's only Saturday, come Sunday, I have a date with my princess.

We'll go to the zoo, spend a buck or two, she'll smile from cheek to cheek.
It's only Saturday, come Sunday, it will make my whole week.

We'll grab a burger, just to please her, then we'll tell a joke or two.
It's only Saturday, come Sunday, I'll be happy just like you.

I'll tell a story, about a girl named Lori, she'll ask me questions and try to rhyme.
It's only Saturday, come Sunday, we'll have a real good time.

I'll take her home, then feel alone, she'll hug and kiss my cheek.

It's Sunday evening, and I'll be looking forward till next week.

Yellow Mass

Sun up, frost is gone, a shimmer on the lawn.
Nervous am I, the school bus near, a kiss, and now she is gone.

Taken away by a yellow mass, to learn what must be taught.
That two plus two equals five and answers the questions sought.

Herded in like cattle, with seeds planted deep,
The lesson plan accomplished; they're following like sheep.

Taught to respect their elders and people that represent power,
While grown-ups steal, rape and murder, every waking hour.

Eight hours could not come sooner, greet her with a hug,
Discuss the merits of the day and cleanse her with my love.

Dreams

She dreams of a world where butterflies rule,
Where roses fill landscapes and evenings are cool.
Where porches are full of familiar faces,
That tell other stories of magnificent places.
With streets void of litter and unwanted hate,
Where the grass grows freely with white picket gates.
Where the sun shines daily without any rain,
Where people are noble and never spread pain.
Where the colors of fall exist year around.
Where the leaves paint a picture once they land on the ground.

Kite

In the park the laughter slows down, as the day becomes the night.
The breeze has shown its strength, as she has lost her homemade kite.
And the only sound you will hear, is the cry from deep within,
But Pa Pop is there to hold her, and wipe tears from her chin.

The kite, it is long forgotten as she takes hold of her spoon,
Anticipating ice cream that will be arriving soon.
The chocolate fills her tastes buds, she grins a country mile.
And as Pa Pop gazes at her joy, he breaks out in a smile.

He walks her to the front door and to the second floor,
He gives her one final hug as she opens her bedroom door.
He walks back to the street, beneath the moon's bright glow,
As she yells, "I love you Pa Pop," from her bedroom window.

With flashlight in his hand, the nighttime sky so dark,
He drives back to the place, where they were playing in the park.
And as she's softly sleeping, in the middle of the night,
Her Pa Pop's search is over as he found his darling's kite.

Ode to Jayliana

Your little plastic figurines, all lined up in rows,
You have worked hard to put in line, as your imagination
grows.
The world inside that you create, for your solitary time,
Brings a tear inside of me, greater than any words or rhyme.

Sitting with your open book, with the words pouring off the
page,
Brings me so much happiness, no machine could ever
gauge.
And the times that you get mad at me, because I am acting
strange,
I only do it to make you laugh, and that I will never change.

The times when you get sad and down and want to cry a bit,
I'm crying just as hard inside, and that I'll never quit.
In the evening I often wonder, if you are sleeping tight,
And are you feeling comfortable, throughout the long dark
night?

In the morning when I see you, and we sit at the breakfast table,
My favorite time of day it is, me, you and cartoons on cable.
Then it's time to catch the bus, an exchange of I love you,
Now you're on your way to school and now I'm feeling blue.

Bias

In the land where Montague knows no bias and the air flows in shades of lavender lives the hearts of little ones. Their wooden figurines capture the adventures of the day. No electric box to bend the mind. No ancient texts to divide. They think for themselves. No generations to proselytize their blank canvasses with wretched thoughts, filth and hate. No bullets to take them to heaven. Only rainbows, flowers and butterflies color their world.

Cake

Candy canes of silver and gold.
With plenty of flavors that never get old.
Adventurous stories told from lips,
From a green and purple hippopotamus.
Flowers of pink as tall as the trees,
With petals that sway, creating a breeze.
And the river flows with strawberries and cream,
As the fish swim along in your fairytale dream.
With a wonderful place where nobody cries,
Where everything sings, even butterflies.
And the beaches are made of marshmallow sand.
You can eat it if you want, right out of your hand.
And you enter a field made from blueberry pie.
Enough to feed you, your friends and I.
As you wipe the berries, off your face,
You decide to name this magical place.
With your dream finally ending and a smile between cheeks,
you hope to repeat it for weeks upon weeks.
The name you give it is the "Land of Cake,"
As your eyes softly open and slowly awake.

Story

Fall deep into sleep now, your dreams need a stage,
Another day finished, a turn of the page.
Your innocence laying along on a cloud,
Forming a rainbow and singing out loud.
The playground of pink sits on candy of cotton,
Your stress from the day is surely forgotten.
The magical swing that you are sitting upon,
Takes you on journey to moon and beyond.
You swing through the stars saying hi to each,
A beautiful spirit that only they teach.
A visit to Nadar, a planet of grape,
The yummiest planet that you ever ate.
The cosmos is calling with roses of red,
But time to return to your comfortable bed.
Your eyes softly open with memories grand,
You reach for your teddy on your nightstand.
You sit up in bed in all of your glory,
Can't wait to see Pa Pop and share your great story.

Seasonal Garden

Lie down, oh little one, and close your eyes tightly. Escape to a world known only to you, where mermaids dance to your favorite melody and the smell of cotton candy fills the air. Angel's above sprinkle you with love, guiding you through your magical land. Arrive at your seasonal garden where just a blink of an eye can make it snow, change the color of the leaves or pour hot sun down. Tonight, choose the snow and play in the fluffiness. Catch the flakes on your tongue. If you get too cold, blink your eyes and the sky will warm you. Pick from the rainbow of berries overhead, flavor at your desire and from the river of strawberry. Enjoy the caterpillar, though beautiful, the butterfly flies away. Dream hard, it cannot be taken from you. It is your permanent solace from a cruel world.

Nature

Just remember in any time of need or sorrow,
Always choose the way of the flower.
You can learn from its instinctual strength,
Letting go of the old petal, growing a new.
I tell you this from experience,
And remember to water it, everything on Earth relies upon
something else.
Never succumb to anyone who cannot plant and nurture,
Always take in its fragrance, a gift given freely to soothe.

Conqueror

With no bow in her hair, she climbed the hill to tall grass for the first time. The sun behind her lighting the way, warm breeze keeping her hair out of her eyes, even though her small hands brushed it away, a habit she had become accustomed to. The soft terrain made it difficult at times to steadily plant her feet, so she would take the form of a puppy she had learned from her childhood novels and use her hands and arms to advance. Upon reaching the top, her determined look turned to that of a conqueror, happy with smile. Her tiny hand reached out for mine. We walked through colorful meadow, enjoying her new-found world. From the aged bark that stood mighty remain solely in our memory, and in these words, more vivid and compelling a story than any camera can tell.

Of Love

Bloom

Under cold ground of winter, where flower clings to life, you will find a soft smile planted, distant from my face, poised for springtime. When the first ray of sun sprouts bud of green and petal of yellow, so too will my smile bloom. And like the fragrance that finds its way to you, so too will my smile.

Shade

Meet me where the books are made, in the soothing redwood's shade,
It is there we will find a chapter full of muse and masquerade.
The clever words will ripen as they are lifted from the page,
Digested in the mind's vast world performing on its stage.

They will carry us through space in time, through voyage upon blue sea,
Through spirit gained on rainbow's edge from dawn's antiquity.
To the stars we will go on sturdy wings, feathers soft on hand.
Across the fields where heaven rests on quiet solemn land.

We will read the words until cover's end, story, rhyme and pun,
'til journey has been satisfied and shade gives in to sun.

West

Soft yellow words on tip of tongue so eager to escape,
Ears on lonely mountain peak sit patiently and wait.
Yellow fades to pale remorse, its dying painful hue,
Avalanche of hidden thoughts that never see the truth.

Flagrant inhibition from broken steps not taken,
Jewels and gems with dull appeal, their shine was lost in
lesson.
Shelter crashes through the wind, my spirit left in space.
Leaves have turned from green to brown, my world has lost
its grace.

Enchanted reminiscing circulates through day,
Of those I choose the painful ones, strength has gone away.
The smile I often think about, has taken to the west,
Unspoken words full of tears, lie dormant in my chest.

Slowly Fade

Crafted words on paper torn, prepared for shattered heart,
Criticize the midnight talks, the thieves of restless art.
Spoken from experience, of anguished mass appeal,
Numbed by preexisting terms, nerves no longer feel.

Tainted verbs spoken strong, pierce through tired skin,
Truth is buried deep in mind, cemented strong within.
Covered by eternal force, of questions never spewed,
Memory is lost again, reality became unglued.

Half-thought lies of yesterday, surface from my land,
Materializing right and wrong, from depths I understand.
The burning star slowly fades, to realm I have never known,
Pilot's course has vanished thin, perception slowly grown.

Silhouette

Silhouette dancing on the backdrop of time, details never seen, only a vague outline each holding a different color flower, bright in their glory swaying effortlessly, passed to the one they are destined to. The only emotion realized is that of an enlightened silhouette smile. A single orange one, my favorite color still circulates, passed through hands, still as beautiful as the day it bloomed, soft petals, strong stem, waiting with open hand.

Different

I knew you were different when the butterfly landed on your nose. You giggled. You did not flick, swat or shake. The tickle pleased you while the butterfly rested. And when it finally flew away, your eyes followed it with a gentle smile while mine followed yours.

Scene

Beautiful landscapes on a canvass torn,
Silver and gold that has never been worn.
Time spent in shelter away from the pain,
Umbrella broken, getting wet in the rain.

Throat swells from truth, bond has been broken,
Regrettable thoughts from words never spoken.
Flowers of purple that once filled my scene,
Are withered to root, grass is not green.

"Shout if you can hear me," said the raspy butterfly.
"I hear your spoken cadence, through your lonely sigh."
Was the last time that I heard it, the wings no longer spread,
Spoken word not heard, written ones not read.

…Now the rain stops, the fragrant primrose is carried to me.
To my left, a garden full of butterflies showered in silver
and gold wings.

Mongolian Beef

Mongolian beef and butterflies,
Under the beautiful shelter of Dominican skies.
A perfect evening for a perfect date.
I have cooked your favorite. Here is your plate.

Last Breath

Your empty vase sits near the ledge, dear,
Balanced perfectly with nothing left to hold.
The flowers once delivered to my doorstep,
Have wilted into memories of old.

The table sits with crumbling legs tormented,
Countless splinters scattered across the floor.
No meals at night for it to kindly serve us,
Past conversations hung outside the door.

Bluebird sits lonely at my window,
Broken wing from neglect, moment of despair.
It struggles with its last breath taken,
Its spirit carried off with fragrant air.

Our painting on the wall no longer sees me,
Face faded; colors bland from fallen grace.
Moonlight through the drapery hits the ledge, dear,
Your smile has left the room without a trace.

Above the Trees

The streets are lined with memories past,
Where the cold wind blows, where nothing lasts.

And the fields are full of leafless trees,
Where the bitter air will never please.

And when you look up to the endless skies,
All you hear are ancient cries.

Then the howling wind cuts through your face,
And all you have thought seems out of place.

Then a moment of silence before the tears,
And in the distant mist a butterfly appears.

Closer and closer its wings are seen,
Blue, red, and orange and magnificent green.

With wings so large and strong to fly,
You climb aboard and wave goodbye.

Above the trees where the air is pure,
You fly away to a far off shore.

It is there you learn to laugh and sing,
Under the shelter of your butterfly wing.

Pictures

I planted your white tulips yesterday, the ones that you had asked for,
The ground seems healthy and rich, I wish I could have planted more.
It was right around the time when the wind picked up, the trees, they were shedding their leaves,
With my squinted eyes and chapped cold hands, I dug upon painful knees.
As I cleaned the dirt from under my nails, a smile came across my face.
A little pain now will be worth it later, when they bloom under the sun's grace.

As you sit in your concrete garden, with no grass to plant a seed.
You needn't worry or shed a tear; I'll plant whatever you need.
The garden is yours even though you're not here, you can see it at any time,
You don't have to call or send a letter, just appear with no reason or rhyme.

And if you can't, I understand, I'll send pictures whenever you request.
You can look at them as if you're near and choose the one you like best.

Until they bloom, I'll protect their home with all my power and might,
If a strong wind howls and the rain is strong, I'll shelter them through the night.
When springtime comes, and birds sing their tunes and the melting ground turns green,
I'll be standing right there, with focused eyes, until the first bud is seen.
I planted your white tulips yesterday, the ones that you had asked from me,
The ground seems healthy and rich, I just wish you were here to see.

Waltz

Valiant ghosts reappear when the sky screams your name.
Visions in the atmosphere point fingers, finding blame.
Clouds' formation overhead takes shape of kindred smile.
Illusions of a perfect waltz take over for a while.

Chinese fan above the trees dancing west to east.
Cloud has changed to helpless frown, a vision I like least.
Expression of the dancer's waltz has turned to one with pain.
Umbrella shredded in my mind, the cloud floods me with rain.

Tide

If you have drawn your line in the sand, then I will pick
another beach.
You can build your sandcastles there and I will be, out of
reach.
I enjoy the sand, but only one grain at a time.
You like grabbing all of it, with no reason or rhyme.
As you toil in your work where your cities of sand are built,
I will be on my side, fearless and free of guilt.
And as the day grows longer and the moon above with
pride,
Your castles will be washed away by the high and mighty
tide.

Allerednic

Well, her slipper broke on Wednesday, not her favorite
night.
You see her legs had become swollen and the glass was just
too tight.

She went by Allerednic, turning everything all around.
To her the sky was beneath, as she looked up to the ground.

And in the moment of that fracture, a tiny piece did land.
Puncturing her labored skin, blood pouring down her hand.

The sight to others, quite painful, some said quite alarming,
While she sat there in her red-stained dress, waiting for her
Prince Charming.

She sat there till the sun came up, he never did arrive.
The blood had now formed a scab, as she began to cry.

She sat for days and wondered, why he never did arrive.
You see, he was off chasing dreams, and trying to survive.

Five years later she had changed, the glass she has forgotten.
Now she wears upon her feet, slippers made of cotton.

Reclusive

He was not lonely. He just liked being alone. Neighbors were fooled by his reclusiveness. Behind the bland entrance to his home, void of any color, with front door paint chipped and faded from the 1970s, lies a home full of brilliant life. Once inside, the aroma will lead you back to the kitchen where he performs his favorite hobby. French pastries, the finest Asian dishes, cuisine from the Caribbean, foods from everywhere around the world including good old-fashioned American comfort food are all prepared here with vigor and passion daily. Who would have thought? Next to the kitchen in his library, every book he has ever read is housed perfectly in its place on a shelf. He has traveled many places over the years in this room. He has visited the land of Oz alongside Dorothy. In fact, one time he knocked the witch over before she could set the scarecrow on fire. He has been everywhere in the world and outside of the world. It's all right there on the shelves. Up the steps and off to the right is his favorite room, full of pictures and memories of his family. An old, faded picture of his parents rests on a dresser. He looks at it every day to remind him of how special they were and what a wonderful childhood he had. Pictures of his children cover the walls. Those pictures take him back to all the family vacations, milestones and celebrations that they shared. And then on a special table sit pictures of his late wife and a bottle of her favorite perfume that he sprays every day to further remind him of her. He sprays the bottle and just stands and stares at those pictures. Some days he smiles. Some days he laughs. Some days he clinches his fists in anger and some days he stares at them stoically. But no matter the day, when done looking, a tear or two always find their way down his cheek. He is not reclusive. He has much to do behind those four walls. Cooking, reading and memories.

You

I've seen preachers kill with words for fun.
I've seen babies being born with guns.
I've seen doctors kill with their drugs.
I've seen white men kill but not called thugs.
I've seen horses fly in skies of blue.
I've seen leaders lead with words not true.
I've seen ancient scripts ruin lives.
I've seen queen bees lose their hives.
I've seen children growing up too fast.
I've seen old people judge their past.
I've seen kings and queens lose their wealth.
I've seen healthy people lose their health.
I've seen fields of violet when I sleep.
I've seen people smiling but inside weep.
I've seen poor folks help one another.
I've seen rich folks shun their mother.
I've seen blind men see without fear.
I've seen men with eyes that can't compare.
I've seen unborn children with no chance.
I've seen childless couples in a trance.
I've seen fights and wars that never end.
I've seen politicians that don't care when.

I've seen many things, this is true.
But I've never seen anyone like you.

The Sweater

The first thing I remember on that day ago a year,
Was the nightfall came so suddenly when the sun did disappear.
Mother nature gave no warning, as the breeze circled me with fear.
While the sky turned the deepest shade of gray and a chill rose up in the air.

An unconvincing knock upon my door was barely heard at all.
There she stood with big brown eyes, a pretty smile and not too tall.
She looked familiar, I had seen her before, maybe somewhere long ago.
I invited her in, she took a seat and ran her fingers though her fro.

She thanked me for letting her in and getting her out of the cold.
I told her I like to live dangerously as she began to roll,
her sleeves with butterfly prints, down to cover her skin.
I asked her where she came from and why she wanted in.

She told me that her sweater was a living breathing thing.
And that all its magical powers, were hidden in its wings.
A fortune telling women had gifted it one day.
The wings of the butterfly on the sleeves would point her in the way.

It sat in a closet for 14 years but washed and folded each week.
Too afraid to put it on, not knowing what it would seek.
Something told her to put it on earlier in the day.
The wings took off and bought her here, I was not sure what to say.

I made a meal, pulled out her chair and handed her a plate.
The conversation lasted a while, neither of us ate.
She asked if she could stay the night and take a long hot shower.
I said, "The towel is on the shelf, I'll check on you in a half hour."

I made her bed in my spare room and offered it for the night.
She fell asleep rather comfortable; I closed her door so tight.
I slipped into her duffel bag, the sweater, I had to know.
My initials on the collar's tag, that I weaved many years ago.

Fade

I have words to share with others from lands afar that you have never heard, dreams on my horizon yet to reveal themselves. The scent of jasmine will still fill the air. The fawn will graze, the brook will babble, and the leaves will change. The space between rest and slumber may be painful for a while, but the mellowing sound of nightfall's melody will comfort. Your favorite color will fade, a new one will paint my future.

October 6th

If I could trim the rose of petal red and cast it to the wind,
With flailing wings of splendid soft, melodic words within.
Soaring through the bitter cold, battered bruised, forlorn,
Withered from nature's plight, surviving, slightly torn.
It would find its way to kindred spirit that rests towards eastern skies.
Nestled below her lashes black, deep within her eyes.

Velvet Throne

The stars come up; my feeling goes down.
At nighttime I wear a stagnant frown.
My crooked mind my crooked soul,
Been a long time since I've been on a roll.

You say you've been there, to this distant place,
Surrounded by scorn and eternal disgrace.
Well, I bet that you have never felt alone,
While you sit there upon your velvet throne.

I'll sleep when I'm ready but not too soon.
I'll sleep with no pillow under the falling moon.
And if the rain pours down. I'll just get wet.
Your memory vanishes but I'll never forget.

My ocean's tide has risen above.
My hands of time are covered with a glove.
The feelings I have I've never owned,
While you sit there perched on your velvet throne.

The sky's color fades from blue.
You've taken the air from it too.

It suffocates slowly, its birds can't fly.
You watch closely, as the wings have died.

It's hard to see the flightless cries.
It burns a graveyard right through my eyes.
It's not only me, I am not alone,
While you sit there lounging on your velvet throne.

The snow has fallen but it doesn't cover.
The road is traveled by a distant lover.
It leaves a path of footprints small,
Too hard to trail and not worth it all.

I take my shovel through I'm out of whack.
I dig too deep, and I've hurt my back.
I drop to my knees, and I let out a groan,
While you rest in leisure on your velvet throne.

My ship has landed on a golden shore.
The things I've felt I don't feel anymore.
My pen and paper are my two best friends.
They pick me up when there's no means to the ends.

I keep my ink full and my thoughts on loan,
As I stare at the pictures on my phone.
I'll be okay, I'm not alone,
As you sail away on your velvet throne.

Woods

When the skinned knee heals, you will smile and wander the woods again.

When the storm passes, river subsides, you will travel the hills again.

When your broken heart heals, you will smile and begin to dream.

When your sanity flees from loss, you will carry the pain onward, of which you won't recover.

And when you close your eyes upon last breath, you will think of the woods and smile.

River's Bed

Past the final star where the tired rest and the wind takes
pause from flight.

You will find my stretched out patterned thoughts that swim
in majestic light.

Their motion that rolling hill, swaying through limb and
mind.

Written in a stellar book, that has no sense of time.

The words, they pour from river wide, that floats in lack of
air.

Come drown in depths of lovely language, of love, truth and
despair.

Meet me in this treasured place, your shackles you must
shed.

I'll pat you dry and cover you upon the river's bed.

Paths

I have cleared a path of thick thorny brush with bare hands painted in blood, cracked from elbow to fingertip and closed eyes. From ground and mind, it was removed. It will remain barren through the cold of winter, a period of reflection. Come spring, it will dance with yellow, orange and red flowers, buzz with bees, butterflies and feed the thirsty hummingbird... On ground and in my thoughts. You can visit both as you wish.

'Til Teardrops Form

There is a chair that sits on open porch, won't you sit on it
sideways please?

You can stare all evening 'cross the field of memory, beyond
the swaying trees.

When the breeze picks up and cool moves in, you can dress
in blankets warm.

The smell of nighttime's loneliness, hovers 'til teardrops
form.

With your eyes half shut and breath felt deep, you can hear
echoes of a nursery rhyme.

It will soften your bones and soothe your spirit, take you to
a simpler time.

When the hoot owl sings to the moving winds, you can find
your way inside.

And admit the night is hard to conquer, but at least you
know you have tried.

Bouquet

Happy to receive her bouquet of flowers, what a nice gesture Jacqueline gathered. In another world, Emma waits for water and bread. Grateful for the strength from it, she plants more seeds. Certainly, in due time, another bouquet created, for someone to receive.

Butterfly's Rainbow

If a rainbow gray had formed above lacking color in the sky.
I'd lend the perfect shade of green that lives within your eyes.
The violets that you walk upon, I would cast up towards the bow.
I'd share your heart of red with it, so everyone would know.

The orange from your orchard's trees, with lemon, yellow too,
I'd harvest your creations aplenty, with berries made of blue.
The indigo I'd capture from the hue around your soul,
Its soft and warm identity would make the rainbow whole.
When colors fade and rainbow ends, they'll make their way to you,
Waiting for the next great rain for me to take anew.

Dangling

Through subdued shade of gray, I view the world. Determination present for a journey not started. My heart measures distance with recurring ache the further she travels. Dangling toe in water never realized, afraid of serpent's bite and not finding my way home. So, she travels further, and I write perched at edge of sea, with words never fast enough to meet her distance.

Exit

Gather what is left in the pond of the day, the much-needed water you'll need.
Waste it not on a flower dead, it is time to plant a seed.
Open the door to the earth below, dig until your fingers hurt.
Bury your treasure of forbidden quest and cover it with stench-filled dirt.

Quiver inside as you walk away, tremble with fearless plot.
The love you knew to set you free, in time will be forgot.
Harness the shade within the field, the ruins of lovers past.
Vomit their spirit from stomach to ground, their memory will exit fast.

Goddess

I will meet you beyond the cloud, far from the raging sea. It's there we'll hover beneath the stars. We will plant flowers red, and green; they'll strive in dreams of spring in garden spread from moon to sun. On my wings we will travel through, taking each one into breath and exhale fruitful bouquet downward for others to enjoy. Meet me, goddess of flowers.

CPSIA information can be obtained
at www.ICGtesting.com
Printed in the USA
LVHW082052230822
726590LV00014B/427